JOURNEY TO
ENLIGHTENMENT

Rodney Groves

• JACARANDA PRESS •
TEMPE, ARIZONA

To Order Contact: Rodney Groves
P.O. Box 201 • Mayer, AZ 86333
(520) 632-4469

JOURNEY TO ENLIGHTENMENT
Copyright ©1998 Rodney Groves, Mayer,
Arizona.

Jacaranda Press, a division of
Roberta Burnett Communications
607 E. Loyola Drive
Tempe, Arizona 85282-3834
602 966-4900

Printed in Canada

Journey to Enlightenment
ISBN 1-879046-03-2
Library of Congress BL350.385 Eastern
religions & philosophy

Book Design: Lynlie Hermann

DEDICATION

To

Herbert E. Groves, Jr.,
my father,
for his example
and
his inspiration
1928 - 1989

&

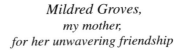

Mildred Groves,
my mother,
for her unwavering friendship

&

To my wife Patricia Groves,
for her many years of
dedication and
steadfast commitment

ACKNOWLEDGMENTS

I want to acknowledge here the many individuals who have inspired and prompted me into spiritual thought—which has eventually brought about the creation of this book. Among those are Stephen Mitchell for his translation of the *Tao Te Ching*; Daisetz Teitaro Suzuki for his book *An Introduction to Zen Buddhism*; Thomas Byrom, Jack Kornfield, and Gil Fronsdal for their editions of the teachings of Buddha; David Schiller for *The Little Zen Companion*, a collection of modern and ancient Zen thoughts; Robert Pirsig for *Zen and the Art of Motorcycle Maintenance*, as well as the masters—Henry David Thoreau and Ralph Waldo Emerson—for their love of and fresh perspectives on Nature. I especially wish to thank those ancient scribes who worked with diligence and fortitude to bring us the ancient writings and teachings of Taoism, Buddhism, Hinduism, and Christianity which are the foundations of this book.

I also wish to recognize here my family and friends for their encouragement and comments on this material, as well as my editor and publisher, Roberta Burnett, for her dedication to the clarity of this book's thought and the quality of this rendering of my manuscript.

CONTENTS

Introduction

Long before I had heard the word "enlightenment," I was building the foundations for my own personal spiritual enlightenment. I discovered that my greatest peace, and my greatest sense of wonder, came from being in nature. As a young boy of six or seven and even throughout my youth, I would take many solo excursions into the forests surrounding the homes where I lived with my family, throughout Upstate New York and later in Northern Arizona. There, in the quiet of the deep woods, I discovered the magic of life and nature and an appreciation for its beauty and power, even while it defied my comprehension. As an adult, I had discovered and pursued religious teaching with fervor for many years. Without realizing it, I was on the path to discovering my own natural intuitive awareness while learning the teachings of Jesus of Nazareth and other philosophical teachers. What followed were many years of practicing meditation in the form of "nature meditations." I also began practicing other forms of meditation such as emptying the mind of all thought, and meditations upon wisdom and scripture, particularly The Lord's Prayer. For a brief period, I investigated the philosophies of Hinduism and Taoism, finding much of value in these philosophies as well. A year spent hiking throughout the mountain ranges of Korea and becoming acquainted with the Korean people brought me an appreciation of Oriental life and Eastern thought. Here I discovered Zen, The Way of letting life be what it is — *naturally.*

The awakenings that I have had communing with nature and contemplating the ancient teachings have become the foundations for my understanding about life. The major religions and spiritual philosophies admonish us to simplify our lives, to recapture the innocence of life, to live life fearlessly and with respect for others. Beyond that, they awaken us to the understanding of divine eternal love and of the oneness of life, the connection that we all have to each other and to the divine essence of life. It is necessary that we learn to connect to the natural world to fully be aware of this connectedness to the Divine. In the natural world, life is most real and reality is there experienced most profoundly. In nature there are no pretenses, politics, fantasies, or lies. There is only that which *is.* In the awareness of nature, with a Zen state of mind, there is only the *Now.* When a person experiences the *Now* of natural reality, the presence of divine intelligence becomes overwhelmingly evident.

We all have glimpses of enlightenment from time to time, moments where we feel at one with life and when we have a heightened sense of the presence of the divine intelligence that flows through life. As we share our personal spiritual experiences, we are able to help each other realize the meaning of these experiences. In this we help each other attain a better understanding and a more vivid awareness of life.

What follows in the next few pages is a glimpse at two personal experiences of simple enlightenment. They have been included in this book to help you develop an understanding of enlightenment, what it is, how you may recognize those moments of enlightenment in your life, and how you may help yourself to bring about those moments more frequently.

Simple Enlightenment

All my life—and I assume it is so with most people—I have sought that which satisfies the deepest hunger within me. I continually search for the natural beauty of life, that which speaks to me of my connection to the Divine. I needn't look far. I have come to the realization that we are always surrounded by natural beauty, which is the essence of the divine intelligence of the universe, even when we live in the middle of the city.

Natural life is all around us: We must learn to focus on it and to recognize it. My attention is directed to the ivy that has made itself at home on the wrought iron fence at the end of my patio. It's now over six feet tall and continuing to spread its grasping, leafy tendrils over the entire fence. I noticed it as a small sprig poking its form out of the soil of the flower bed. When it emerged, it was about six inches away from the wrought iron. I also noticed its consciousness. It reached across the six inch span of distance to begin wrapping itself —a conscious effort—around the fence. As it grew, not only did it wrap itself up the wrought iron bar, it wrapped itself symmetrically! The spacing between the wraps was consistent between windings, almost identical. In that moment, to me, this observation was an awakening! I began now to see the presence of intelligence in all life forms. Where before I had taken for granted the existence of universal intelligence, I now saw it as the "presence of God," and with that moment, I began to notice this presence all around me.

Recently I spent some meditation time in the mountains, at the 8500 feet elevation in Northeastern Arizona, deep in an area of densely distributed ponderosa pine. I meditated upon Hawley Lake and its inhabitants. With my mind cleared of most thought, I observed the life around me. As I stopped the ramblings and analytical trappings of my mind, I noticed something that to me was unusual. Time slowed to a crawl and then became nonexistent as the life around me became magically alive! Nothing physical had changed, but I became aware that I was totally surrounded by eternal life. In this life exists intelligence, an intelligence that is divinely connected, that is One (or as the Zen monks say, "not two").

Another awareness then occurred to me. All of this life was created out of a sense, a divine sense, of Love, especially for me. Suddenly my connection to life, my own personal and divine essence, the love that God has for me, my place in the universe, all became real and apparent to me.

As I sat in silence and with my mind quieted, I observed the activity around me. The water, the core element of life itself, filled the lake. Acres and acres of it, giving life and providing home to millions of life's creatures, plant, animal, insect, fish, microbes, ad infinitum. As I looked at the lake, I saw the ducks, wild and free. Comfortable on land, water or in the air, they were unencumbered by any need to do anything or to be anywhere. Slowly and relaxed, they floated along the current of the water, occasionally dipping their beaks deep for a bite to eat, their tail feathers sticking straight up to the sky. Observing them, I felt connected to them and to their simple way of being.

Then I noticed the fish—trout I assume—that were instinctively driven to feed: It was as though they all received the message simultaneously that it was feeding time. One by one they emerged to the surface of the water, each creating rings of waves at the point where they poked their snouts out of the water to catch a low flying gnat or water scooter. At first these rings appeared only while the fish fed on the bugs close to the water's surface. Then the fish became aggressive and playful as they began to splash and to jump out of the water in pursuit of their prey. I became keenly aware of this activity and all of the activity of life surrounding me. On the distant shore an angler whipped his fishing rod back and forth, casting his line across the water to catch a nice plump rainbow trout for an evening meal. The insects, the fowl, the fish, and the human—this all became an orchestration for me, a visual composition of the activity of life.

Turning my attention away from the water, I became aware of the vegetation that surrounded me. In all their naturalness were the trees, small sprigs of young trees barely making their entrance into the world alongside the stately ponderosas. Sentinels, these pines had been there for years and years beginning as little seedlings and before that seeds that hung on another tree. Here they overlooked the hills, the rocks and the lake, and all the other vegetation and creatures of the forest.

Even the grass beneath my feet began to radiate with life and intelligence. I felt overwhelmed by a sense of divine love and intelligence surrounding me. The entire forest, the lake, the sky, the clouds, the air, the people, the plants, and even the insects became connected, and so they became alive with a new meaning to me, purposeful and filled with love and intelligence. Everything became significant. Everything had a reason for being. As I reveled in it all, I sensed divine love embodied in the creation of all of this. It was more than my limited human mind could dare to comprehend. Again, it was overwhelming.

This simple walk through a perspective of nature brings us to the purpose of this book. The purpose of my writing, as I see it, is to describe my inspiration, to describe my sense of my own enlightenment, and by these to help awaken within you, the reader, a sense of your connection to the Divine Intelligence in life. Its purpose is to help you to see another perspective that may enable you to satisfy the craving deep within you, the yearning of becoming connected to your divinity. Perhaps you are already there, and perhaps you have had these experiences without understanding them. By knowing someone else's experiences, we may come to perceive our own a little differently and for what they truly are.

Life is a journey through a wonderland. It requires us to develop the ability to recognize this wonderment. It exists all around us.

JOURNEY TO ENLIGHTENMENT

Preface

This book is a blending of spiritual inspiration found in the observance of the natural world and of spiritual thoughts from around the world. It is written with a loving wish to bring readers to an increased awareness of

❧ Who we are

❧ Why we are here, and

❧ What we can do to bring ourselves closer to living our lives with divine influence and purpose.

From world philosophies I have borrowed the following concepts:

❧ Practicing and living life in unconditional love

❧ Being in harmony with the universal order of life

❧ Working for positive change lovingly and with

divine patience

❧ Being totally accepting of what life brings us

❧ Living life in total faith

❧ Living in the Now

And overriding our human activities are two other, even more fundamental concepts:

❧ The spirit of divine intelligence, literally existing in all life

❧ That all life is inherently connected, so that what we do as individuals affects the whole, even on the smallest and seemingly most insignificant level.

Everything changes.

Change makes life the exciting wonder that it is. The ancient Greek teacher Herakleitos spoke these words to his students: "A man cannot step twice into the same river." This image underscores the reality of change. The river changes constantly and inevitably. Moment by moment the river changes as the soil and rock erode away with the constant movement of the water. Vegetation takes root as it transforms itself, turning from seed, to plant, to flourishing plant, where it produces seed of its own that then turn into another plant. Microbes and organisms, along with the fish and crustaceans, live and die in this eco-system, producing offspring of their own as the cycle of life continues on and on. Like the river, life changes constantly, and so it is too with life beyond the river. In our own bodies cells die off and new cells are born every millisecond of our lives. We renew and become new.

Spiritually speaking, each of us is the caterpillar changing into the butterfly. Within its eggshell, the embryo of the eagle becomes the eagle. The human evolving into the higher spiritual being arises from humanness to divine being. Daily occurrences change us. As our awareness of life grows, our priorities change, and so we change the way we perceive life and the way we make decisions; hence, our lives change forever.

Paradoxically, much change that occurs in our practical lives is beyond our means of control. As much as we would often like to, we cannot change the world to fit our preconceived ideas of how our lives should be. It is this inability to change the externals, or rather our inability to adapt to their forces, that causes so much of the difficulty and turmoil in the world. In individuals, this inability to adapt causes frustration and sadness. Often this leads to social problems and personal health problems, often serious ones. We must learn to adapt, to change that which we can and to accept that which we cannot, and to accept it wholly, without regret.

JOURNEY TO ENLIGHTENMENT

Spirituality and Harmonic Centeredness

Spiritual awareness requires consistent diligence. We change in matters of degree. If we seek to be spiritually connected to the source of all life, all love and all intelligence, we must put the fiber of our being into a mode to receive the connection, just as one would tune a radio to the proper frequency to intercept radio waves. If we have the dial askew, if we are receiving more than one station, we need to adjust it in order to get a clear signal.

Known and accepted throughout the medical world for many years is the idea that the mental state of a patient affects the healing process. Many believe that our mental states and our attitudes cause illness to occur in the first place. Certainly, our spiritual state is very significant. It influences our mental and physical health. Many people throughout the world believe that a person's inner harmony and their harmonic centeredness with the universe create good health. The more a person lives a life in focus of the universal laws of unselfishness, love, consideration, and compassion, the better their health. Inherent within us is the need to live in tune with those universal laws. When we don't, we produce inner conflict that needs to be resolved.

Changes in the human spirit occur incrementally. When we change physically, we go through a process of metamorphosis. Just so, we do that spiritually. First is a recognition of our ego. Liberation from our ego involves restraint and redirection of our thought processes. The less we allow the ego to dictate our thoughts and actions, and the less it is the sole focus of our lives, the more we come closer to spiritual completeness and spiritual beauty. In other words, to mature spiritually means that we take control of our fears, even our most subtle and almost unrecognizable fears. The changes of life are accepted as inevitable, and we learn to love life as it is, whatever it is.

Such awareness means that we love life and accept unconditionally the divine influence in life. In addition, we train our egos to give, for a state of unconditional love seeks no compensation for the good works it renders, neither in this world, nor in worlds to come. In the Mahayana Buddhist tradition, we learn to give because it is necessary. Expressing ourselves through the act of giving brings a sense of satisfaction to the core of our being when it is done as a gesture of love. Detaching ourselves from our own wants and desires, in and of the material world, brings the purest satisfaction to our spirits. When we are able thus to draw ourselves closer to the spiritual side of our being—that is, the side which operates out of love instead of the ego—we become able to feel fulfillment and harmony. When giving is done as a true gesture of love, we hold no expectation for any reciprocation. This love is called "unconditional," the purest love of all.

Materialism

We are all materialistic, at least to some degree. We live in a material world and we need material things to survive. We all desire to acquire material possessions, of some sort, in order to make our lives on this planet bearable and more comfortable. Acquiring material goods applies to the dynamic of our spiritual balance. The problem comes, however, when the acquisition of material goods dominates our lives. It is then that our inner harmony is disrupted because we are spiritually out of balance. The difficulty comes in being able to keep our material acquisitions in perspective as they apply to the complete picture of life—eternally.

Most of us are so submerged in the quest of obtaining what we think will make us happy that we fail to recognize that which truly will fulfill our lives and bring us boundless joy. Jesus of Nazareth put it in words that explained it so very vividly, "Seek first the Kingdom of Heaven and all else will be given you," and, "Do not put your treasures on Earth where thieves will steal and moths corrupt." Over the centuries and even since these words were delivered, we have been culturally convinced that we can buy our way to happiness. For a short time acquisition does have a satisfying effect. Like the junkie, however, once the initial satisfaction wears off, we begin looking for our next "fix." Depending upon how entrapped we are by our need to possess, we may stop at no extreme to satisfy our wants and desires.

Each of us is, at times, another type of person, one who is genuinely and earnestly in search of the answers to the questions that burn at the core of our being: "Why am I here?" "What is the purpose of life and death?" "What is the purpose of the experiences that I have?" Instead of being caught up in the cycle of material possession, a person finds joy in simple things. The fragrance of clean air on a crisp country morning, a newborn infant taking its first breath, or the beauty of a peach blossom opening for the very first time.

What is significant about these simple joys is not only in the pleasure that their occurrence brings to the individual. There is significance in the understanding that a person is participating in these timeless miracles, in the basic essence of life, in effect since life itself began.

Materialism quite definitely has its limits. It is one thing to have necessary possessions for our reasonable survival and comfort in the physical world; it is another thing, entirely, to love those possessions. We must be aware of the possibility of losing our possessions at any time; we must prepare to detach ourselves from them should they become lost. Losing them tests us: When we lose these possessions, we will immediately see how spiritual we are and how materialistic we have become.

Our greatest material possession is our physical body. Each of us is a spiritual entity that inhabits a physical body. This statement contrasts with the common belief that we are physical bodies that have a spirit within us. On the contrary, as spiritual entities we have put on our physical bodies in the same way as we enter an automobile or a backhoe: We want to increase our mobility and our ability to perform functions in the physical world; we want to use this physical form to learn eternal lessons. Without our human physical form, we consist of pure energy. This energy is a cognizant, aware force, an energy of pure love and intelligence. When we act fearfully, that is, act with our egos, we obscure this love and intelligence. We then become who we think we are in this physical world, rather than who we truly are.

Acquiring Enlightenment and Universal Perspective

One of the most difficult experiences in human life is probably the acceptance of who we are. We all have experienced growing pains in our lives, times that we would rather not remember because they are an embarrassment to us. Facing the reality of who we are and who we have been may be considered by some to be equivalent to plunging oneself into "Hell." Sometimes, however, it is necessary to put our egos through hell in order to emerge stronger and purer in our thinking. We must accept our short comings and see them for what they are, obstacles to be overcome in attaining a higher state of being.

When the ego is surrendered, no threat to our inner being exists. When the individual realizes that his or her nature is pure love and intelligence, and not the ego (which is simply a manifestation of a collection of our fears), then that person realizes that the physical world, with all it problems and difficulties, is only a temporary condition that human beings must endure and can and should learn from.

Acquiring enlightenment and increasing spiritual awareness is not easy. The truth is, these must be regained continually for they can slip away and disappear with the slightest change of focus. In order to acquire them, the desire must be foremost in our minds and hearts continually. Then comes effort: We must dedicate our lives to this purpose if we wish it to be so.

People are all very protective of our very fragile egos, of the perception that we have of ourselves and that others have of us. Equally, we are protective of our perceptions of the world. All minds, to some degree, operate in dualism and everyone reaches conclusions of what is "good" and what is"bad." It is necessary, however, to rise above this dualism. Included in this is the subtle fear of not being valued, accepted, and of being found unworthy by others. If a person wishes to truly be in touch with a core of full potential, then that person must risk exposing his or her ego. We must learn to love unconditionally, trust completely, and to risk our ego fearlessly. It is our lifelong task to peel away the illusions and uncertainties and thus to achieve the universal perspective that frees our spirits and empowers us through the awareness of being one with the universe and being totally connected to the great source of love and intelligence.

One of the most difficult tasks that we have is to learn to see ourselves as something other than the center of the universe. We are all aware of this fact on a physical level of understanding, but on the spiritual level it is quite a different story. In our culture, each of us feels that his or her own personal needs are the most important and should be administered to first, before the needs of anyone else. When we become truly enlightened, our own personal needs diminish and the needs of others less fortunate become a priority. Enlightened, we perform our life-tasks for very different reasons. While we do not lose our individuality, we see ourselves as part of the whole. Our individuality becomes stronger than ever, and it benefits the whole rather than a part. It no longer aims at serving our own ego-driven, self-centered needs but refocuses on serving the needs of the whole.

Our Divine Purpose

Many among us see themselves as brought into a world of turmoil to struggle for survival. Because human beings are physical-spiritual entities, we work to provide physical comforts for ourselves. At the same time we try to understand our purpose for being. We want to be useful and make the most of the time that we have here. We all struggle to fill the spiritual void within ourselves. Driven by a need to satisfy that emptiness, we search for meaning to life.

A universal theory is that each of us has a purpose for being alive on this planet and that every event has a reason for its occurrence. Human beings have the problem of trying to phrase our understanding of these occurrences in human terms and in trying to relate these occurrences to our lives as we perceive our lives to be. We all have our perceptions but those perceptions are very limited at best. The terms we use and the perceptions of life that we have are limited by the nature of our limited understanding of the universe, both physically and spiritually. It is necessary, therefore, to simplify our thinking to allow intuition, the intelligence of the spirit, to reveal truths to us, truths that we will recognize because they touch the very depths of our being.

We are here to fulfill two basic spiritual needs: The need to face our fears (the fears which comprise our egos) and the need to tap into our true being, the unlimited reservoir of love within us. When we are aware of that true being, we will affect positively all who come in contact with us. Those who fully accept all that occurs and have the unending ability to spread love and joy to others are literally "angels in the flesh." Their first priority is to please others, not themselves. Humanitarians, they do all things, no matter how mundane and seemingly trivial, with a sense of dedication to others, with unconditional and non-expectant love. The greatest persons who have lived in this world are those who have opened our understandings to the potential within ourselves, collectively and individually. They have shown us that facing our fears and being totally true to ourselves puts meaning into our lives and makes the struggle of survival a purposeful and important endeavor. Those who influence our lives most positively understand an underlying principle: What occurs in life fulfills a greater purpose than what is humanly perceptible. They accept this precept in faith and go forth spreading love and positive energy wherever they go. These unique individuals emanate positive energy through a sense of dedicated purpose, love, and effortless confidence. Within them lies divine purpose. Being in their presence elevates the spirit, giving you confidence and a heightened sense of your own purpose. Pettiness and selfishness dissolve into a sense of fulfillment and peace.

Naturally each of us is capable of becoming and being these "higher spiritual beings." In fact, at times and even as spiritual novices, we have flashes of it. At these times, we are these highly elevated beings; we give of ourselves unselfishly and unconditionally with love. It is in these moments that we live our lives for the benefit of all others and for the higher good. When someone is enlightened, he or she is able to recognize that all of us are angelic beings in the transformation of realizing our angelic essence. To an enlightened person, small acts of kindness and love become significant. People who were strangers before suddenly become spiritually connected to the enlightened person. Joy is created in experiencing this recognition.

The Power and Glory of Love

Unconditional love is a great force; quiet and serene, it is all encompassing. Like the ocean tide, its force cannot be controlled once it is unleashed. Its influence is far reaching, causing dramatic change wherever it is encountered.

In order to have love, and in order to experience it, we must find it first within ourselves. We can't receive love from others until we have learned to give it from the deepest core of our own souls. Giving love must be foremost, permeating all our being, not just in one special circumstance, but love must be exercised in all that we do.

Love is strength. Its power comes from being able to let go, to let it flow freely. We cannot attempt to control life, and we cannot attempt to control love. When we realize this, we also realize that life and love are one and the same. In life and love we must allow the miracle of the Spirit to take root within us and guide us. To experience its strength and power, we must be willing to endure all things with the understanding that any experience will bring us closer to realizing our divine essence and connection to all of life, whatever the experience is. We must not judge the experience as "good" or "bad," for to do so is an expression of the ego. We must simply experience each moment and learn, not as this lesson pertains to our temporal physical being, but as it pertains to our eternal being. We must, therefore, live to express unconditional love in all experiences.

All creation struggles with and in the physical world, and that applies to the simplest life forms through to the most complex, the human being. Typically we are slaves to the physical world and to the wants and desires of our bodies and egos. Living in the physical world, dealing with the problems of life, and confronting even our most subtle fears, gives us the ability to become aware of life's purpose, of our divine eternal nature, and of our connection to the Divine Intelligence of the universe. This spiritual growth, this awakening, is inevitable. We can either seek and accept it willingly or it will be thrust upon us by life, whether we are willing or not. In any event, we will learn from the experiences.

JOURNEY TO ENLIGHTENMENT

JOURNEY TO ENLIGHTENMENT

THE MEDITATIONS

MEDITATIONS

To love your life and to live every moment of that life fully, completely in the Now and with unconditional love for all of creation — to process your life in this way is to honor your life in the highest degree.

Take joy in doing the most menial tasks. Do them with love. Do them completely in the Now. To be focused so that we may be totally aware of the Now is to savor this very moment of life. To do so is to realize and act upon life's sacredness and to begin to be part of it.

Each of us was born enlightened. It is when we return to that pure state of mind, having total faith in life and the divine essence of life, that we become re-enlightened. People begin seeing life with their eyes and mind wide open. This is the ongoing process of awakening. It enables us to see the world and life with a new vision, as though we see for the first time. It is a spiritual rebirth to a higher plane of awareness that we have occupied in some long past time.

In everything that lives, Divine Intelligence exists. The life that exists in all living creatures is eternal and infinite. This infinite life, this infinite intelligence, exists in all beings, even in the smallest and simplest of life forms. Whether this life inhabits a body or not, it still exists. Infinite intelligence is divine, it is the essence of life.

This thought goes even deeper, to another level. All that exists is Divine Intelligence, even in inanimate objects. All things material are composed of the building blocks of matter, atoms. Within all atoms exists the infinite Divine Intelligence. Nothing exists, whether it is animate or not, that does not have this intelligence within it.

—And deeper yet: Even that which is intangible, which appears to be emptiness, is Divine Intelligence. The air

that we breathe is composed of mole-
cules and atoms; within them is contained this divine, infinite intelligence,
which quite literally exists in all.
Consequently, we are totally enveloped
in this intelligence. The more we
progress as a species in our awareness
of life and what it consists of, the more
evident the existence of this nature
that's divine and intelligent becomes.
Recognizing the divine essence of life
is a matter of recognizing the infinite
intelligence of life.

Be mindful: Life is change and growth. All is metamorphosis. Our condition is as it needs to be at this very moment. When we accept life as it is, no matter what it is at this moment, then we realize the potential of our lives and the power hidden deep within us. Then we can never have regrets. Life is forward motion.

The ego impedes the actualization of our true, eternal, inner being. Through the process of attaining enlightenment, you allow your eternal being, which is pure unconditional and divine love, to manifest itself completely. Then your true self becomes awakened. When that happens, even strangers recognize the essence of your eternal inner being, and respond to it with theirs. In this exchange is the manifestation of our higher consciousness.

We are always moving forward, learning from our experiences, even when the awareness of this learning is not evident to us.

Experience Life: Live it to the fullest with thankfulness and joy. See the eternal and divine infinite intelligence at work everywhere. This is enlightenment!

- To reconnect to life and to awaken yourself to the essence of it, it is necessary to return to the basics of existence.
- Simplify your life.
- Drink into your soul the simple, yet complex beauty of nature.
- Eat the simplest of foods. Slowly taste their complexity.
- Revel in the wonder of creation.

- Your senses will drink all life in when you are truly awakened to its wonder. The immense and unfathomable system of creation is overwhelming.

Put forth your very best effort every day; then let every day be as it will. Put forth your very best effort every moment; then let every moment be as it will.

Seek out loving beings in your life. They will reinforce your quest for spiritual awareness. They will spiritually recharge you, enabling you to encounter the challenges in life with renewed strength and enthusiasm.

Be mindful: All physical conditions are temporary. All grief and sadness result from attaching too much emphasis and importance upon temporary earthly objects and conditions. This idea goes even further — all grief and sadness are the result of our inability to affect the conditions of life as we wish they would be. We must accept life and the phenomenon of change.

We will be slaves to the physical world and to the wants and desires of our bodies and egos unless we become aware of our true being, that which is the essence of infinite Divine Intelligence.

All physical and spiritual life, in this world and worlds beyond, is a process of labor. All living entities must exert will in order to exist. Even the plants—which do have a consciousness—through their own effort, their own will, push themselves to sprout, to grow, and to bloom.

Each of us is the essence of divine infinite intelligence. Our individual intelligence is part of the collective intelligence of the universe. When we sense this, we understand two major concepts:

❧ We are one with creation, and

❧ Creation is not complete without us.

When we realize these as truths, we realize that we are infinite and eternal.

L ove and pain—these are the mothers of creation. Both are necessary for creativity to occur and to blossom. So it is with the creation of our higher spiritual being, our "angelness." Welcome both the love and the pain. They are wings to a higher awareness, to a higher realm of being.

We need all the experiences that we receive in life. Every experience, no matter how joyous or painful, is what we need to transform ourselves to a higher consciousness. To become fully aware of our eternal connection to each other, to the oneness of existence, and to the eternal source of all life, love, and intelligence— to do these things, we must and will experience all that life exposes us to.

One must take the risk of exposing flaws in order to reveal the greatest personal inner beauty. This beauty is found in courage, courage to love, to trust, and to risk one's ego. When we set aside our fears, the essence of our inner beauty shines through us;we become aware of the beautiful eternal being within our flesh and within the flesh of others. Setting aside fears is the act of manifesting "true being."

When you communicate with someone, listen to the feelings that flow from him or her to you. Savor the thought and the feelings rather than only hear the words. To do so is to connect to the other person and to feel what he or she feels. To do so is truly to understand. This is communication at a higher level of consciousness.

Out of any struggle with chaos and confusion emerges the beauty and simplicity of understanding.

You must be willing to lose yourself completely before you can find yourself completely. To attain the deepest awareness and enlightenment, a person must empty both heart and mind—empty them to the very depth of being—of all desires, wants and judgments. It is necessary to surrender the ego to allow the awareness of the divine essence of life to take root within us. In this lies peace and fruition.

Discarding our fears, we realize a direct connection to the Divine Intelligence. Our fears create the feeling of our separateness, a feeling of being alone in the universe.

Allow the essence of the divine love to manifest in your being: Become aware that you—and all others—are not alone. We are united with these others who, like us, are one with the spirit of infinite and eternal divine love.

The time comes when we must stop living for ourselves and begin living for others. We must feel love for all others in every cell, every fiber of our being, for all of us are equals: None are above or below us. We must act upon this feeling, this awareness, with unconditional giving of ourselves, for the purpose of expanding the influence of the greater good.

Life is continuous and eternal. The pains endured in life will not end when we leave our earthly bodies. We will exist again and again in the physical plane where we will experience the joys and sorrows of living in a physical form. We shall do that until such time as we have learned all that we must from the experiences we have.

Necessarily, then, when we are alive to pain and suffering, we learn to accept it as part of the metamorphosis, a growing and transformation that we call "life." When you experience even the normal difficulties of life, remember that eternal lessons are to be learned from every experience. These lessons focus us upon the eternal and infinite intelligence that exists in ourselves and teaches us to recognize it in others.

Earth mother and earth father, your earth child is a spirit of God left in your care. When the young bird has developed its wings, it must fly. Have no doubts: Allow it. Let your heart be at peace with the understanding that this child will experience whatever it must in order to bring awareness of the connection that this child has with the divine essence of life. We all have this connection, and we all seek to become aware of it.

Innocently, we are all teachers, we are all students. All humanity, indeed all of creation, is our teacher.

It matters not what you have done with your life up to this point, only what you do from here on. It matters not what you have been in the past, what matters is who you are at this moment. Who you are in the Now is directly connected to how receptive you are to the influence of the divine power of love in your life. To dwell upon your past, to wallow in your sorrows, or to focus on temporary earthly desires is to serve only yourself. To serve others is the fulfillment of your divine purpose.

Ego has doubts, but your eternal being simply is and does, never questioning its purpose, its abilities, or its future. Your essence of being operates simply. It does what it must and leaves the rest to the divine influences of life.

The underlying assumption here is that whatever happens to anyone benefits that person's eternal being. Your own eternal being receives its awareness and guidance from the eternal source of life, love, and intelligence; therefore, the being within you knows what to do and how to do it. When you live in this state of faith, you live by acting accordingly.

Each of us at our central core is a fountain of love, a love that derives from a divine and eternal source. This divine love flows through us. Just as water must flow to remain pure, so must love. Therefore, we must always be giving our love away with acts of kindness, large and small. Love must be allowed to flow freely to be at its purest.

Sometimes what we want is not what we need. The powers of the universe all work and labor toward our spiritual growth. And so, the spiritual growth of each of us is the result of the combined forces and efforts of the entire universe and the Divine Intelligence of life.

We are not of this world: We are visitors here to learn lessons required for the development of our eternal being. We are spiritual entities inhabiting a physical body. We are here in the physical form temporarily to learn how to reconnect to universal power, the source of all life, and to each other. We must practice unconditional love habitually until the reality and understanding of this concept becomes woven into our innermost fabric. At that time, *practicing* and *living* unconditionally will be totally indistinguishable, and we will live in love and service to each other. Our lives then move to a higher level of eternal being.

Do not fear a violent storm. Experience it without fear, but with divine faith. In this experience, you will grow in spiritual strength.

All of nature, except humankind, acts on instinct. For us it is necessary to analyze the merits of our actions and to be the best that is within us. To do less is to act as animals. We must live our lives as beings with higher consciousness, the beings that we actually are.

When you experience pain in life, go into it, experience it fully. Do not hide from it. Experiencing it will make you stronger in the end. It is the combination of love and pain that facilitates change and metamorphosis. Pain is necessary for growth.

When you let go of what you want and allow the eternal and Divine Intelligence of the universe to manifest itself in your life, when you accept even that which disrupts your tranquility and seems painful at the time, then you receive the greater good, the more precious gift.

To truly understand, we must transcend conceptual thinking. We must learn to see life from a different mind than the one we have used to view the world and life until now. We must take upon us the Eternal Mind that sees with a universal perspective. To do so is to transcend space and time. To do so is to see into eternity and to become infinitely aware.

We are *all* destined for eternal greatness — because the infinite and eternal divine love that guides the universe knows no bounds.

Ego will attempt to use spirituality for its own benefit. The greatest accomplishments can be achieved when a person surrenders ego and self to the process of any task completely without regard for material or spiritual reward.

To realize our place in the universe is to realize that we are all children in our understanding of life and of the continual divine influences on life.

When you lose your spiritual way, put away fears. Amazing and profound discoveries can be made when you are lost.

Each moment of life contains something special and unique in its experience. Live in the Now: Discover what that special experience is.

L ive an enriched life. To do so, love unconditionally and without expectation for others' behavior. Face life's challenges fearlessly and with a heart full of faith. See every day as one to be used for attaining a higher awareness. Empower others, for doing that is an act of unselfish love. Live life in the moment, aware of the Now. Be aware of your eternal being and of your connection to all life. Such awareness is not limited to the contemporary but transcends eternity. It is a connection to all that exists, all that has existed, and all that will exist.

Sometimes it is necessary for us to have confusion in our lives, to challenge us to discover our deepest feelings, and to reconnect to the divine essence of life.

When you encounter the poor, see them as yourself. Give them the same kindness that you would give to anyone you know. We must love and serve all people. When we act in this way, those we connect with may realize that when they also love and serve others, they will experience a transformation. In these continuing cycles, all our physical, mental, emotional, and spiritual needs will be met.

In surrendering ourselves totally to the infinite intelligence and wisdom of the universe, we are required to relinquish all our fears, concepts and our idea of separateness. In this, we are able to allow the infinite intelligence of the universe to manifest within us: We then become totally empowered. We become one with the universe, with all creation, and we are able to tap into its infinite powers.

Enlightenment cannot be made to happen: It simply must be allowed to happen. Just as baby birds learn to fly for the very first time, enlightenment occurs when we are able to let go of our earthly bonds and trust in the wisdom and infinite intelligence of the universe.

An infant has no awareness of self but is filled with delight at the wonders of all that their senses reveal. The infant is simply *being*, and in the act of simply being is complete, whole, and perfect. The infant is one with the divinity of life.

When you create, do not see yourself as the creator; see yourself as at one with the creation in progress. When you lose yourself in the act of creating, that act is a perfect state. The highest degree of creativity is the result of being attuned to the divine spirit and letting the divine spirit work through you. Being this attuned allows your creativity to be its very best. And so, we must learn to set aside our egos and let spirit show itself in our work. This is talent, the characteristic a person manifests when he or she puts heart and mind in tune with the divine essence of life, accepting all creativity that is given, with a heart full of gratitude, humility, and love.

To be loving and charitable in thought and deed is to be in harmony with the universe and one with the divine source of all life. To be such must be the focus of our existence in the physical plane. We must be charitable and express loving kindness in all that we do. When we express unconditional loving kindness, we help to bring others to an increased awareness of the divine essence of life, the pure love of life, and to the existence of the divine essence within them. The individual comes to an awareness of his or her own true angelic nature, passing on unconditional love to others and causing transformation of the world we live in.

While we serve others and the needs of the world, we should not expect that others are here to minister to our wants and needs. Others are here to find their own path to spiritual growth and enlightenment. Any service they give to us, in the same way as service we give to them, should be done out of unconditional love.

Every molecule in the universe is in a state of transformation — continually, and so it is with our spiritual essence. We are always changing and growing.

You may have seen summers before, built fires before, or been kind to a loved one before, but each time is a new visiting of that activity. Each is a new moment, and you have never been in it before. In understanding this, you become more aware. You rebuild your life in each moment.

W hen you are with another, be fully present. Experience the moment as if it were the only one that ever existed. This is a moment of experiencing divine love. To be distracted is to rob that other person of your attention; to be distracted detracts from the love shared in the moment. The interaction of two spirits is a sacred and potentially rejuvenating affair — so long as we interact from our core and not our ego. To pay complete attention to the moment is to feel its full sacred value and rejuvenating effect.

If you want to see into eternity, learn to see life again through the eyes of a child, which means to see as though you are seeing for the first time. Let your seeing have perfect faith and acceptance of the perfectness of life.

Live in the Now. This is all that is real. Anything else, past or future, is only a phantom, a ghost. Neither the past nor the future exists. There is only the Now. We must truly be alive and aware in the present tense to see the existence of eternal life and love all around us. Just so, we realize our divine purpose and our connection to all life and to the divine source of all life. Live in the Now, love in the Now. When you give love to others, you serve your divine purpose. We have been given the stewardship to administer love to those in the present. Be in the Now!

How can you find the answers to the eternal questions of life if you *only* look outward at the temporal situations of life? Seek that which is eternal and infinite. Look *within*. Seek awareness of your divine essence; then all that you see outwardly, you will see with a new vision.

Recognize the moments of love in your life and savor them. Recognize acts of love and kindness done by others, even when they can barely be seen. To do so, we must be deeply in touch with the spirit of love within ourselves. Internalize these moments of love, letting them live in the core of your being, so that they will serve you in your time of need. In recognizing and internalizing these acts of love that we witness daily, we are banking memories that are sustaining, that carry us through times of stress and emotional drought. The witness of these acts also works to transform us into more loving and charitable beings, most aware of our connection to life and to others. *Then* we are most aware of our oneness with all of creation and with the eternal source of life, love, and intelligence.

When we think of ourselves as apart from each other, that is our misperception. Whether we are aware of it or not, we are always one with each other and with the collective Divine Intelligence that is Life. To be aware of such melding is to be fully aware of your spiritual connection to all other beings and to creation.

To make the world a better place, we must become responsible universal citizens in our thinking and in our actions, becoming "angels in the flesh." Inherently we have this ability. Those who give of themselves lovingly and without condition are the more highly evolved beings in the world. Opportunities are divinely created in our lives so that we can administer to others with messages of hope and love, and to witness our connectedness to the divine eternal source of life, love, and intelligence, and, further, to witness our connection to each other.

The natural condition of your true being is to be centered, awake and aware. All of life's occurrences naturally enact to bring us back to the center. The stresses of life are simply the natural consequences of being out of the center.

Practice patience. Take time to express love and to be considerate of others. You cannot practice loving kindness when you are in a hurry. Love takes time and infinite patience.

When you are enlightened, nothing is ordinary.

Everyone — no matter how poor, no matter how infirm, no matter how destitute — as long as there's an ounce of life within them, has the capability of giving love.

The master is gentle, the master is kind. The master is compassionate, the master is loving. The master is forgiving, the master is benevolent.The master is quiet and serene, the master is trusting. The master is non-judgmental, the master is accepting. The master allows the divine intelligence of the universe to express itself naturally. In this, sometimes the master teaches by his or her example of letting things be. At other times, the master teaches by example in doing good works — not ever, however, mastering anyone else, only himself.

S eek the truth in all places. Find the beauty in all people, in all crea-tures, in all of nature and in all things. When we become aware of truth, our understanding of life becomes clear and pure. When the clarity and purity of life is revealed, then life becomes the most beautiful.

The rose blooms in the garden and is beautiful. The jimson weed also blooms: Beauty springs forth. Wherever Divine Intelligence resides, there is beauty. Divine Intelligence is everywhere: That's where beauty is.

When we give with unconditional love, we increase our possession of that which we have given away.

Life is a constant state of creation and re-creation. We are, and all life is, in a state of being created.

Find an oasis in each day of your life; recharge and reconnect to the love of life, for love is the great healer. Healing occurs when we allow ourselves to love and to be loved.

Seek out moments in which you can simply *be*. Learn to be, simply and with a quiet mind, in places surrounded by nature's eternal and divine beauty. In the natural world, you will experience the awareness of being one with creation.

Healing comes from the divine infinite and eternal source of all life, love, and intelligence. It comes from without and from within. It comes in the form of unconditional love, aligning us with the eternal and infinite power of the universe. When we eliminate our desires, wants, judgments, and fears — thereby surrendering ourselves to the natural healing forces of the universe — the healing of our spirits and, consequently, of our bodies occurs.

In your present state — as you are at this moment without any changes — see yourself as one with the Divine Intelligence of Life.

When you look at people, look deeply, without judgment or analysis. Literally see their eternal essence and the love that abides within them. Take time to know people and to see their eternal connection to you. Let them know that you genuinely care for them. Have infinite patience with them. We are all in need of unconditional love and kindness. Give it freely — you always can.

When you define yourself, you limit yourself. Who you truly are is indefinable and unlimited.

The true appreciation of art comes from being able to feel what the artist felt when the creation was made. So it is when we look at life's creations. If we can allow ourselves to feel the divine love that creates the flower, or any of creation, then we truly commune with the divine essence of life and become attuned to the divine source of all life, love, and intelligence.

On the horizon, we see the mountain, stoic and stately. Its appearance is that of inanimate immovability. When we look more closely, we see that it too is animate, full of life and continual changes, and we see its many signs of movement. We see the mountain in all its beauty as it infinitesimally transforms. We see it as it truly *is*. We have awakened to its reality.

L ove is the basis of all creation. All people are inherently connected to eternal love, which is total, patient, eternally enduring, and unconditionally giving. What we perceive as God or Divine Intelligence is pure love. This love encompasses all beings uncondi-tionally. As we put forth the effort of giving unconditional love to others — thereby fulfilling our divine purpose — we will evolve spiritually to become aware of our connection to the eternal and divine source of all life, love, and intelligence.

When we become enraptured by our own wants and desires, we tend to take the phenomenon of Life for granted. In this state of mind, we cannot see its divine intelligence: It exists all around us as well as within us.

All of us exist at different stages of spiritual development and all of us encounter whatever we must in life to bring about our spiritual growth. The ragged beggar on the street is who he needs to be at this particular moment.

You are who you are for your spiritual development. The eternal metamorphosis is constantly taking place within us all, moving us into a new awareness and to a new level of being.

When you encounter moments of confusion, turn off the inner struggle that comes up within you. Allow the Divine Intelligence to awaken and enlighten you intuitively, the Divine Intelligence which permanently resides within you.

When you are trapped in a state of confusion, remember that this is a temporary situation, magnified by fear. Faith in the outcome and in the divine influence upon your life quiets your fears and dissolves your confusion.

We are much more than we perceive ourselves to be — a million times, a billion times so. The fears contained within our earthly minds, fears that are directly related to our bodies and to the mortality of our bodies, limit the awareness of our true eternal being. When we become aware and fully in tune with the perfectness within us, and when we are able to trust that perfectness fully, we will realize that we are the essence of Divine Intelligence. Being divine spirit, we can and will perform divine works.

Surrender your desire for power; align yourself with the pure essence of the universe and become truly empowered.

Every morning, greet life with enthusiasm but without expectation, for every moment will be what it needs to be in the journey toward the realization of your true being. See each day as a divine gift to be deeply appreciated. See it as an opportunity to develop your awareness, to move closer to the realization of your perfectness, and your connectedness to all mankind and all creation. Each day of your life and every moment of your life is a learning adventure.

All of life — in fact, all of creation — is balance. Living in the physical world teaches us spiritual balance.

See Divine Intelligence at work everywhere. Seeing this way is enlightenment. Seeing this way cannot be made to happen. Seeing this way is simple; it must be allowed to happen. Only when we discard the complex symbols of life and learn to see its naturalness do we live and become enlightened.

Be as fluid as water in your thinking. Cling to *nothing*. Embrace all life and all creation with love.

Our fears create the illusion of our imperfection. We are, every one of us, the perfect essence of divine infinite intelligence. Once we are able to discard our fears, our Oneness with all becomes crystal clear. Your intellect cannot help you become aware of your true being. Your intellect can only tell you of the possibility of its existence. Only through your love of life and your faith in its perfectness can you realize your essence. Faith in the integrity of your life is absolute.

Your true being is joyful and loving, an entity of Divine Intelligence. Seek to recognize your essence of joy and love. Once you acknowledge it, the true being you are will be manifested to you.

The mind is an ocean. Don't be afraid to explore these waters and the possibilities that you find there. Take care, however, in your use of its possibilities. The thoughts we have are as varied and as numerous as the creatures of the seas. We each are fishers in our own oceans. Just as the fisherman does not keep all the fish tangled in his net, so should we not keep all the thoughts that flow into our conscious minds. Keep only those thoughts that are choice. Throw back those that are not.

Be aware that all we consume comes from a living entity. Life must consume life in order to exist. When you bite into an apple, recognize its divine, living intelligence.

Unconditional love must exist in our every inhalation and exhalation. This is the way to be fully in tune with the divine essence of the universe. Every beat of your human heart must echo with unconditional love for all humanity, for all creation, for all existence. Do all that you do from the center of your being with a love that does not expect reciprocation. In that lies the awareness of your true being. In that lies enlightenment.

Be aware that Divine Intelligence is at work in every moment of your life, guiding you to a greater understanding than you now possess. You act and the Divine Intelligence influences your life to return you to the center of being, the point of enlightenment.

Live lovingly and patiently in the Now. Have faith that the past was what it needed to be to bring you to this present awareness. Have faith: The future will be what it needs to be to take you to the next level of understanding.

The only pure love is unconditional love. Our purpose for living is to learn to love life unconditionally, accepting all the highs and lows life gives us. To learn to love ourselves and to love each other unconditionally — these are equally important endeavors, for unconditional love is the spiritual reinforcement that each of us yearns for and needs.

This need varies in us. It is never constant. We must, however, recognize this need in ourselves as well as in others, and we must be prepared to give as well as receive.

Believe in the inner purity and goodness of others; you will find yourself realizing your eternal connection to them. When we believe that others are a threat to us, we live in fear. Fearful, we operate from an ego state, ignorant of the harmony of the universe, and so, fear fuels a feeling of separateness. When we believe in the purity of others and accept them as we accept ourselves — that is, as pure beings — our own eternal essence will recognize the love-essence of others. The realization of our connectedness to each other will be obvious, and we will be at peace, centered, and aware. We will then live in pure love, the essence of our true being, instead of in our ego. When we live in this state of mind, we transform ourselves and the world around us.

The simple yet overwhelming beauty of a flower in bloom gives perfect evidence to the existence of Divine Intelligence and to the harmonious essence of the universe.

A perfectly quiet mind is essential to awaken us to our divine essence. Intuitively, we all have an awareness of our divine essence and its presence in all creation. We must still our thoughts to bring this intuition from the depth of our beings, from our subconscious into our conscious minds. With quiet minds, we are then enabled to receive the messages of inspiration and spiritual direction that come from the source of universal love existing within us.

It is when you divest yourself of the fear of *not being* that you learn to be what you truly are.

The most beautiful symphony is comprised of single notes played with perfection. Our lives are our symphonies. Learn to play each note of your life with perfection. You will do so when you play each note with the purest love.

Each of us has but a partial understanding of the workings of the universe and of the Divine Intelligence that creates and orchestrates the universe. When we accept our own limited understanding, we can then accept others, knowing that they too are growing.

To learn to love without expectation and without possession is a step in the liberation of one's being. In the state of deep love of life and of all creation, we experience the ultimate freedom.

The clear, cool brook speaks to me
of the Divine Intelligence of life.
— Do you hear its song?

The essence of life is spiritual evolution. Each of us evolves. We are connected to each other, individually and collectively, as living organisms. We evolve to a higher awareness individually; at the same time, the whole of us evolves. Consistently, we all evolve into a higher life form. As we become more aware of our connection to each other and as we practice loving kindness unconditionally, our evolution accelerates.

Nourish the world with your wisdom and enlightenment. It is a natural occurrence, gentle and without force.

Living life is awakening to a new level of being. All is process.

The way you view the world is a direct reflection of how you view yourself. If you want to change the world, change your perception of yourself. When you feel the need to change the world, soften. By softening, you will manifest the Divine Intelligence.

Music, with all its variety of colors, shapes, and forms, when created and performed from the purest love harbored at a person's core, is a vehicle that will take us to a new awareness, to a higher consciousness within. Music is essentially an expression of the composer's and performer's higher consciousness, and so, when we are attuned to that, it becomes a healing power. Experience this. Seek out its beauty and power. Enable yourself to be transformed.

In the garden we call Earth, we must sow seeds of loving kindness and inspiration. We are all gardeners of spiritual nature, recreating Eden. In our garden, we will collectively reap what we collectively sow.

Most of our time here on Earth is spent living with a feeling of being disconnected, spiritually apart from all other beings. Without being aware of it, we stand on the outside of life looking in. Enlightenment brings us to a new perspective and shows us how to live life from within, connected to all life and to divine love and intelligence. When a person looks at the world through eyes that see from an enlightened mind, everything takes on a sacredness. Then life becomes most meaningful.

We may see ourselves as separate from others, but our eternal lives and our spiritual essence are interwoven, just as are the threads that make the finest silk cloth. The idea of our separateness is an illusion created by our egos.

If an act you perform does not satisfy the core of your true being, of what value is it? Experiences that satisfy move you into expressing your true essence. You become what you always were, Divine Intelligence.

The harmony of our world, of our societies, and of our families will only occur when we begin to teach certain things: We must understand our priorities, which are forgiveness, compassion, and respect for ourselves and others. We must also know, at our innermost core of being, and must teach that collectively these priorites form the foundation upon which all harmonious interaction is built.

When you look at the creations of nature, look beyond the physical into their essence. See the infinite consciousness that resides there. This consciousness is Divine Intelligence. And so it is when you look into the mirror: Divine Intelligence exists in all creation; the essence of it exists within you.

Enlightenment is without confusion or the struggle of process. It is as peaceful as fallen snow or a flower's opened bud. It is an awakening, an acceptance of all that is.

Consideration and loving kindness require long enduring patience. When we practice these normal human behaviors, we are at one with the universe and in touch with the core of our eternal being. When we are in touch with our eternal being, the forces of the universe are aligned within us; through them we are able to use the power of this alignment for the achievement of promoting the greater good. In doing all that, we fulfill our divine purpose.

Serve your divine purpose by per-forming acts of unconditional love. Let this love manifest itself in all that you do.

Divine love and intelligence is all around us and within us. It is manifested in all life. It is present in all life forms and exists in all living things. It is the force which guides the universe and resides even in the simplest molecule.

Can you imagine existence without the presence of love and intelligence?

In all its brilliance, the sun rises to begin the new day. We have faith that it will and expect it. Just so, we must have faith in the perfectness of life. We then become confident that all occurrences in our lives benefit our eternal being and that all things are as they need to be.

G ive love and then peace will occur from without and from within.

🍃 Think thoughts of love.

🍃 Live thoughts of love.

Be aware that all acts of violence and frustration are simply manifestations of our fears. Look deep and slow to see them, for they are subtle and clothed in other names, jealousy, resentment, envy, and greed — and even the fear of not being recognized and valued by others. Negative emotions always come from basic fears. Dispel your fear and you will dispel your life's negativity. Experience the eternal and infinite reality that is your life as it is. Live all of your life in love and faith. Experience joy when you live this way.

Humility and a sense that no beings are inferior or superior to each other are always necessary understandings if a person is to remain in a state of awareness of the eternal essence of life. If a person compares his or her own enlightenment to another's, no enlightenment exists.

In the process of living and interacting with others we experience the greatest risk to the tranquil state of our minds. Here, in this interaction, we experience our greatest growth, our greatest joy.

R educe your life to its simplest terms. In such simplification, you will find freedom and joy of the spirit. Trust in life's perfection. Simplify all you do and think. Instead of trying to exert your will on others, deal with others with enduring patience. Instead of being wrapped in materialistic accumulations, live your life clothed in divine purpose. Then act — with this awareness as the basis of your living.

When you dissolve all symbols from your mind, all ideas, all concepts, all preconceptions, all words; when you quiet your mind and see nature from your position of naturalness, then your reality becomes most vivid. The colors of everything, the smells in anything, the textures of all become more apparent. Your life simply becomes more pure.

Your perfect eternal essence is One with the perfect eternal essence of all life. Trust in this belief and you will step into an awareness that will transform you and the entire universe around you.